10X

YOUR INNER ROCKSTAR

The Ultimate Playbook to Unlocking the Power of Your Emotions and Taking Action Fearlessly.

Leisa Jenkins
Be You, always !!

Leisa Jenkins

10X
YOUR INNER ROCKSTAR

The Ultimate Playbook to Unlocking the Power of Your Emotions and Taking Action Fearlessly.

Abundant Press - Las Vegas, NV 89107 www.AbundantPress.com

Ordering Information & Quantity Sales: Special discounts are available on quantity purchases by corporations, associations, and others. For details, contact the publisher. Orders by U.S. & International trade bookstores and wholesalers at: info@abundantpress.com. Printed in the United States of America- Library of Congress-in-Publication Data. Please note: This book was put together very quickly for a conference, so if you find errors, like spelling or grammar, please send us an email. Thank you.

Title: 10X Your Inner Rockstar
Sub-title: The Ultimate Playbook to Unlocking the Power of Your Emotions and Taking Action Fearlessly
Author: Leisa Jenkins

1. The main category of the book — Personal Development, Relationships, Business
First Edition, First Printing 2-15-2020
ISBN: 978-1-948287-14-2

To Get FREE Access Additional Bonuses Visit:
10xYourInnerRockstar.com

LEGAL DISCLAIMER

The information within this book, website, program, process, and/or document is intended as reference material only and not as medical or professional advice. Information contained herein is intended to give you the tools to make informed decisions about your wellness, lifestyle, and physical and mental health. It should not be used as a substitute for any treatment that has been prescribed or recommended by your doctor. The information within this book, website, program, process, and/or document must not be construed as a medical, therapeutic, or psychological treatment, nor are any such claims made.

Every reasonable effort has been made to ensure that the material within this book, website, program, process, and/or document is true, correct, complete, and appropriate at the time of writing. Nevertheless, the authors do not accept responsibility for any omission or error, or for any injury, damage, loss, or financial consequences arising from the use of this material.

The authors, promoters and publisher are not healthcare professionals, and expressly disclaim any responsibility for any adverse effects occurring as a result of use of the suggestions or information herein. This material is offered as practical, current information available about disease and health management for your own education and enjoyment. If you suspect you have disease of any kind, it is imperative that you seek medical attention. It is also recommended that you consult with a qualified healthcare professional before beginning any dietary or exercise program.

By accepting this information, you agree to hold Leisa Jenkins, her associates, partners, and affiliates free of liability and damage, and you agree to proceed on your own free will. You and you alone are solely responsible for the results that you produce. Do not continue unless you fully agree to these terms and conditions.

10X
YOUR INNER ROCKSTAR

TABLE OF CONTENTS

Thank you for showing up for yourself

DEDICATION

To my husband who has always allowed me to be me. Who has allowed me to up late to accomplish everything I set my mind to. A man who has supported me through my crazy ideas and my ALL-IN personality. A man who has seen me up and down through every battle. A man who has worked hard for our family so I can follow my dreams. A man who had made our family what it is today. A man who has sacrificed so I can use my gifts that God has given me to serve the word.

To my kids who set my path right by being born into this world. Without them I would not be the mom I am today. You are all perfect in all your ways. You are exactly who you were created to be and don't ever let anyone change that about you. A special shout out to our Butterfly Emma. We love you so much! #turnersyndrome

To my parents who gave me the stories and experiences in my life so that I can serve people even more than I ever thought possible.

To all the mentors, coaches, and leaders that have been part of my life who have believed in me, pushed me and loved me for who I was created to be.

To my clients who have given me the continued desire to fight for them each day and to stay with them through every storm so they can 10X their Inner Rockstar.

Thank you for investing in this book and10Xing your Inner Rockstar.

ACKNOWLEDGEMENT

There are many people I want to thank for being in my life and helping on my path. I will never forget the greatness I have had in my life or the people who have sacrificed to help me on my journey. There are hundreds of people that I have come in contact with that have made a lasting impression on my life and impacted where I am today. I could list hundreds of names, including many in the community that you might know, who are also forging their path to greatness, but I want to acknowledge one person in a big way. From the moment this book started to become reality, she never left my side.

Her name is Jeanne Hamra. She has lost just as much sleep as I have. She has edited more stuff for me than you could ever imagine. (That's not her specialty – she is just really good at it.) Jeanne is a Rockstar coach who impacts people's lives everyday with her programs. We have teamed up on many projects, and I am honored to be working with her every day. She is my number one advocate. She has been through my programs and has personally gone through the same process you are getting ready to read about. She is the Rockstar she was created to be and shows it every day with her family, her clients, and our programs. She has believed in me since day one.

She has seen me up and down through heartache and failure and with all of that has never given up on the vision that people everywhere could be impacted by the same principles we will teach you.

She knows, just like me, that sometimes in order to succeed it takes great sacrifice to see things through.

I am acknowledging her today because without her this book would not be in the hands of thousands of people. Without her supporting me, staying up until all hours of the night, jumping on the phone 4 times a day, executing this book, I would not be where I am today.

Find those people in your life that believe in you and want to see you succeed. People who know who they are and are ready to 10X their Inner Rockstar and be who they were created to be. Thank you, Jeanne, for your dedication and hard work to seeing this book and program to the end, so together we can impact the world.

FOREWORD

By

Rob Theiss - Business Owner

A story of hope - written by a client

Before you read how I have been impacted by one person who has never given up on me, I want you to know that everything is possible for your life. One woman showed me that through her gifts and her dedication to being who she was created to be.

Leisa Jenkins changes lives.

This is something I know from personal experience. I have seen her relentlessly positive yet realistic attitude and action-oriented approach toward working through deep-seated issues pay real and lasting dividends in people's lives.

At the end of this book you will find testimonies from several of the many clients Leisa has helped overcome their inner obstacles and move past them into a brighter more confident and happier future.

If you will allow me, I will share some of my own journey, a path I would not have found without her help. Indeed, without her unique influence I would not be here sharing this with you today…and I may not be here at all.

13

My Yesterdays, as Leisa once called them, had taken the shy, high-strung, emotional personality I had grown up with, and through the alchemy of time and a failed marriage, dysfunctional post-divorce relationship, painful breakups and an emotional breakdown, had twisted it into a volatile, bitterly frustrated, hopeless mess.

My psychologists over the years had added other terminology...Severely depressed, co-dependent, explosive temper...suicidal. I struggled to keep up my outer facade of a relatively normal, functional person, but inside I felt utterly lost. I felt hopeless. I had been alone for years and no longer believed I could love or be loved by anyone. My faith had faded and I was watching the years of my life disappear with nothing to show for them.

I was also struggling to find help for my ex-wife, who was burdened with physical and emotional issues of her own. I was sure there had to be someone besides the cold, disinterested medical specialists who were turning their back on her time after time. When I took a chance and called a different kind of doctor, the woman who took my call was so kind, so warm, so caring and compassionate that I felt a glimmer of hope.

At the end of the call we had made an appointment and she then asked if she could pray for me and for my ex. That phone call changed my life. That woman was Leisa.

My ex blew off the appointment, as usual, but I decided to go myself. In our first session, Leisa stunned me by looking me in the eye and offering a sober assessment. She had seen right through my facade in only a few moments.

She saw what lay behind it and told me what would likely happen if I didn't take action and make a change. I did not want to believe it but I knew she was right.

In the weeks and months that followed Leisa taught me more about myself and why I was acting the way I did than I had ever learned before. I honestly came farther in 6 months with Leisa than I had in 15 years with my psychologists. She taught me to recognize my emotions and their causes and how to manage them before they got out of hand. I learned to see life with clarity, perspective and to recognize and defuse the Circle of Crazy that had controlled my life for years. She taught me it was ok to feel good about myself and to enjoy life without being saddled by guilt, doubt and regrets. She convinced me to come to church with her for the first time in decades and I have found a renewed relationship with God.

After all the years of being alone she told me with confidence that when I was truly ready, the right person would indeed come along. I confess I did not believe her then. I do believe her now. Out of nowhere I have met a woman who feels like she is made just for me.

I can actually say it...I am in love.

It is amazing to me how far I have come, and I know I would not ever have gotten here if not for Leisa. Let her help you. In this book you will learn to see yourself and your emotions differently. She sees a pathway for you where others just don't. With her help you will see that path for yourself.

In these pages you will read Leisa's own story.

Honestly...for someone to experience *those* yesterdays and not be crushed by them is inspiring in itself. For someone to take those experiences and use them to help others out of *their* darkness is truly remarkable. This book offers a look into a real way forward from whatever you are struggling with.

Leisa Jenkins can change your life. She has changed mine.

Rob Theiss

Business Owner

Supporter and Advocate of Leisa and her desire to impact the world

INTRODUCTION

You are being introduced to the most important book you can read to 10X Your Inner Rockstar. Welcome to a journey that will get you back to be the person, leader, coach, parent, or individual you were created to be. This introduction is different than most.

You are being introduced to a resource that will show you what you must do before you take action. Slowing down and focusing on the necessary "inner-action" is what will propel you forward and 10X YOUR INNER ROCKSTAR and YOUR LIFE. YES, this is about YOU! I want you to know HOW this book will help you!

You picked up this book for a reason. Take some time and determine why you were drawn to it. Why do you want to 10X Your Inner Rockstar?

Fast Track Rockstar Connection questions:

- What will my outcome be?
- What is the purpose in diving into my emotions?
- What promise am I making to myself?
- What actions will I take to make this book come to life for me?

This book serves several purposes.

- First, it will help you determine whether your emotions are propelling you toward or holding you back from being the Rockstar you were created to be.
- Second, it will help you begin to understand the processes in your mind that control your day-to-day life through your emotions, motivation, and decision making.
- Third, it will help you get rid of the things that are not serving you.
- Fourth, you will learn to take actions that will honor who you are and help you 10X Your Inner Rockstar.

A note from Coach Leisa Jenkins.

I am excited that you decided to show up for yourself and take a stand for who you are and who you want to be. You are on your way to taking your life to another level, and you will soon discover that you are truly just one action or step away.

Get ready to peel back the layers of your emotions so that you can take action to achieve your hopes and dreams, even if you have not been able to achieve real results in the past. It doesn't matter where you are in your story. This book will help you overcome whatever has been standing in your way.

I have discovered how to unlock the mysteries of your mind, retrain your brain, and fuel your life in a way that helps you get back to the person you were created to be.

If you are ready to be the Rockstar you were created to be, then give me an "Oh, Heck Yeah!" Dive in with me, unlock your brain, get off the emotional roller coaster (sometimes referred to as the "Circle of Crazy"), and be the Rockstar you know that you can be!

Leisa
JENKINS

WARM UP GPS

This GPS will help you navigate your way through this book so you can play to WIN!

How to use this book and make it effective for you.

1. Read this book chapter by chapter.
2. Work through the Rockstar Connections questions at the end of each section. They are designed to get you into action, to 10X Your Inner Rockstar, unlock the power of your emotions, and Take Action Fearlessly.
3. Print your Rockstar Manifesto and read it daily! You'll find it in Jam Session 14. Keep it in front of you at all times.
4. Take time to do the work, slow down, and let this book inspire the fearless change you need.
5. Keep this book handy so you can reference the Energy Shots in Jam Session 13 often. This will get you into fast action. We suggest that you work through this entire book before jumping into your energy shots.
6. If you need a boost of hope read the impact stories in Jam Session 16.
7. If you feel like you cannot do this alone or need further help, please reach out to us. We have coaches available if and when you are ready to invest in yourself more and at a deeper level.
8. Congratulations on taking the first step and opening this book so you can Take Action to 10X Your Inner Rockstar and be the person you were created to be!

JAM SESSION 1

The big question:

Why are you not taking action?

Why can't you just get it right?

Why does life seem so hard sometimes?

Why can't you just be who you were created to be?

Maybe you are not in chaos right now, but you might be asking why your best friend cannot get out of a cycle of bad relationships, why your kids don't listen, why your spouse or boss just does not get it, or why your clients are always spinning their wheels.

WHY, WHY, WHY..........

There are many reasons that people will give you as to why they are unhappy or stuck or spinning their wheels. What about you? Are you questioning why you just can't get it right? Honestly, most people are too close to the situation to see the root cause but often tell themselves stories about what they *think* is going on.

You might say or hear things like:

- There are too many opinions.
- My friends don't get it.
- I have too many opportunities.
- I don't have the money.
- I am not smart enough.
- I don't want to be bothered.
- My idea is too ambitious.
- It's too late. I am too old.
- I have failed before.
- I can't take that risk.
- I don't have the confidence.
- I am not like her.
- I have no time.
- I have too much going on.
- What if I hurt their feelings?
- My dad said I will never be _____.
- I have nothing special inside of me.
- I am emotional.

Before I give you the secret, I want you to know no matter where you are in your life, there is a Rockstar inside you wanting to Take Action Fearlessly. It is in YOU! You have everything you need inside of you to 10X Your Inner Rockstar and be who you were created to be, I promise.

Your passions, your strengths, your talents, your gifts are all there--no matter what others say! They are there no matter what distractions have been keeping you from letting that Inner Rockstar come out and play. I believe that life delivers so many great things but also a lot of very unfair experiences and events that could be keeping you from being who you were created to be.

Together we are going to take a journey that will help you Unlock the Power of Your Emotions and Take Action Fearlessly.

This book is different than most books you will read because it includes the steps you need to work through *before* taking action. Yes, I am giving you permission to slow down and stop taking action for a minute. You need to understand why you have not been taking action or not taking the right action. If you want to 10X Your Inner Rockstar, then knowing yourself and your emotions is the most important thing you can do. In my years of serving and coaching others what I have found is that so many people have no idea who they are or how to manage their emotions. They don't know how to take action without fear leading the way.

While action is important, how do you know if the action you are taking is the right action? Most people feel like they are spinning their wheels and are repeating patterns that are not serving them. The books you read today talk about how to have the perfect morning and the 5 steps you need to take starting NOW.

Here is a SECRET: if you are taking those actions with a cluttered mind--a subconscious brain full of unnecessary or unneeded things that may be tricking you and keeping you from living the life you want to live, you are likely taking the wrong actions for the wrong reasons.

25

This is why you think you are making the right decisions but find that you are back at square one, still repeating the same patterns over and over.

There is a chance that you are not taking action because you are being held hostage, manipulated, or controlled by things you aren't aware of. Blind spots! You don't know what you don't know, because you don't know it. Your brain, your emotions, your thoughts, your environment, your relationship, your habits are all part of this big picture in life, and they play tricks on you. You might think you are making the best decision to take action but find out months later it was wrong. Sound familiar? There are things that happen to all of us.

I am here to help you move past all of that so the action you take is the right action and will get you results without getting stuck in the patterns and triggers that keep coming to the surface.

You will discover who you are--not who your environment has molded you to be. Often, we lose ourselves because we are reacting to life events happening around us. Our perception is affected by these experiences meaning you see the world through a lens that may or may not be accurate.

We will dig deep into what is stealing from you and keeping you from being the true, authentic person that your creator intended you to be before life set in. When your thoughts align, your head and heart will be connected, and Your Inner Rockstar will be unleashed.

This book will have you going from your current idea of you to your INNER ROCKSTAR. You will have the confidence to fight for your life and no longer feel like your emotions are one big battlefield.

It's up to you to fight through the storms and dance in the rain. After all, we were never promised that there would not be storms. Happiness and peace are on the other side of whatever chaos, distractions, emotions, and weeds that take away from Your Inner Rockstar.

This world is full of information. In fact, you are drowning in information overload. Slow down and take one bite at a time. Knowing and trusting who you are is the greatest step anyone could take. I know that is not always easy, especially if your story holds you captive. I cannot hold your hand and force you to change, but we can come along side of you if you let us and let you know that you will be ok. We understand that it can be overwhelming to figure out exactly what you need and then Take Action.

I have experienced life on levels that are hard to understand. I am sharing my story in the next Jam Session and you will see that I had to work hard and paddle 10 times harder to be the person I was created to be. Each of you reading this book has your own story that has taken you to a life of serenity or fear. Your life is either taking you away from who you were created to be or revealing more of your true self.

My goal is to set you on the path of greatness by unlocking the power of your emotions, eliminating your distractions, and setting you free to 10X Your Inner Rockstar now and forever.

Are you ready to dig deep into Your Inner Rockstar? Are you ready to fuel your mind with healthy thoughts so you live as the person you were created to be? It is not about where you have come from but where you are going that matters.

Don't let one or hundreds of things in your life define who you are. It is proven that the most important thing is how you are living your life in the moment. It is time to face your fears and head right into the eye of the storm and 10X YOUR Inner Rockstar. You will be more aware of how your life is affected and learn how to change it. We will be here in your corner cheering you on through every chapter and praying for everyone who is reading this book. Your time is now!

Rockstar Connection:

1. Are you managing your life, emotions, and self? Or are they managing you?
2. Are you Taking Action Fearlessly?
3. Are you ready to 10X Your Inner Rockstar, dive into this book, and be who you were created to be?

JAM SESSION 2

Chaos to Beauty - a Rockstar Story of Perseverance.
The Leisa Jenkins Story

Life is hard. Most people understand that they will have to make sacrifices for the things they love, but they often do not understand or know why they often sacrifice the good things in life for something that they really do NOT want. The human psyche is not always easy to comprehend.

I understand the power that comes with understanding why you do the things you do. When that clarity comes, people can learn how to use their own personal story to serve them and the people in their lives. We want people to know they have a chance in this world to discover the greatness within them that is just waiting to be unleashed. We do not want them struggling to figure it out on their own.

You will read in this Jam Session how I grew up with challenges. I understand pain, sadness, and sacrifice. I know firsthand what it takes to lead others while growing a business, raising a family, and battling obstacles along the way. My powerful "WHY" is coaching and teaching people how to overcome the storms of life like I have, so that they can fully embrace the joys of life, just like I have.

My powerful "WHY" gets stronger every day as I set out to prove my story happened for a reason. I will not waste the things that I have been through in life. I need to know my life happened for a reason and that reason is to help you. My biggest dream in life was to build a company that will help people. My story has led to me to my Rockstar life. This story is intense and deep. My hope is that it helps you PUSH harder than you ever have!

From the beginning:

For the last 20 years I have been a wife, a mother, and an entrepreneur focused on serving people. I have seen a lot of good and a lot of bad. I have been frustrated, stressed, happy, mad, sad, scared, and have felt every other emotion you could imagine. I have felt overly responsible for the people in my life: taking care of them, serving them, protecting them, fighting for them, and giving them everything they desired and then watching it crash over and over. My professional journey has been way up and way down: sleepless nights, tears at all hours of the night, many sacrifices, and also winning on every level. But my story did not start there.

My dad was the happiest man in the world the day I was born. He wanted a little girl as he had already had two boys. He ran through the hallway of the hospital screaming, "It's a girl!"

I have held on to that story as I believe it helped me through much of what was coming next. It helped me believe I was important, and I mattered, because what came next was the complete opposite. My childhood was spent overcoming obstacles, living in fear, sadness, and pain. My story is hard to hear, hard to tell, and hard to comprehend. Stay with it! I did!

I am going to give you the short version here. If that's all you want, read the list and move on. If you want to know how this girl writing this book went through Hell and somehow still managed to 10X her Inner Rockstar, then keep reading.

This is a story of perseverance and determination. I hope at some level my sharing the details of my chaos will help you to see what is possible for you. When I was a little girl, I remember sitting in my room singing my heart out knowing that there was something special inside of me and that I could and should never tell people what I had been through--but here I am today sharing it with you. This is, in fact, the first time I have put this on paper.

So here it is:

- 0-4 yrs. old - I was a sick child weighing 13 pounds in and out of doctors' offices
- 0-2 yrs. old - Mice were consuming my crib
- 4 yrs. old - Called a daughter of the devil and crosses being put in my yard

After 4 yrs. old through adulthood

- Head-bursting earaches
- No money, rarely having food, electric being shut off
- Living in flood waters being pulled out by boats
- Sexual abuse, raped by 5 people
- Emotional and physical abuse
- Bullied heavily in school

- Almost killed 5 people in a car accident at 16 yrs. old
- Smoked pot, drank alcohol trying to escape
- Almost failed school and barely made it
- Lost my cousin to a drunk driver
- Lost my grandfather to cancer
- Was the strongest person in every group
- Married at 19
- Graduated high school, got married, had a baby, and bought a house all in one year
- Volunteered, ran a successful business, impacted thousands of lives
- Business partnerships
- Radio show host
- Failure, failure, failure
- Talked about writing a book for 7 years
- Fell down the stairs at my home. Spent 8 months recovering from a shattered ankle--decided to stop playing small
- Finally, wrote my book and kept my promise to myself and the world.

I have never forgotten who I am.

My "why" outweighs any amount of money or material things that I could ever have. I am not the only person in this world with this kind of story. We all have shit. I used to live a simple life scared to make a move, always protecting myself, and living with walls up. I was good at "being good." I was good at feeling like there was more inside of me but thinking that I could not have it. I was good at pushing down emotions and not feeling.

Was I worthy? I worried, "What if people find out who I am or what I have gone through? How will people view me?"

Today, writing this book makes this the day that I am breaking free from that. I can't turn back, and I am not scared. I am embracing what is in front of me and reaching for things that were taken away.

I would let insignificance control me and I never knew what I truly stood for. I had thousands of thoughts in my head trying to figure it all out. I thought I had to do it on my own. That made me strong or so I thought. I tried so hard to block out my childhood. I tried to wash it away--forget that it was part of me. I learned very quickly that was impossible. I made you the bullet-point list because I used to relay my story in a bullet-point list. I did that to keep emotions at bay.

I NEVER wanted my childhood to define me. I did not want anyone to know the secrets inside me. I have experienced life on levels that most have not. It took me years to understand why I had to go through all of that. In fact, it was a question in my head for years. I was not living with it well and fighting it with every step.

Dealing with shame most of my life and feeling dirty, I would lose myself in volunteering and in being involved in everything that would please people. I accepted every opportunity that was in front of me losing myself at every turn and feeling like I was being taken advantage of. I spent half my life looking for acceptance and value.

I survived everyday little by little telling myself that nothing in my life could ever be as bad as what I experienced growing up.

One thing I know is that I am never going back. I lived my entire life in chaos. It's what I know. I thrive in chaos and I have used that gift to impact people around me every day. I did make a promise that my home life would not be that kind of chaos, and to this day, it is a safe haven. I finally feel free and safe when I lay my head on my pillow at night. I am not being chased or held down. I am not being abused and treated badly. I am not being called "same-shirt Leisa" or surrounded by kids laughing at me and pointing fingers. I am not the little girl on the playground no one wanted to play with or the teenager that felt hated at school.

All I did was try to stand up for people. The more I did, the more things came back on me. I had friends that were friends at home but would act like they did not know me when we were in front of people. People were embarrassed to be seen with me. Our family was one of *those* families. My brothers earned us that name.

When I write this story, it brings me back to my roots. It brings up detail I have not thought about in years. The difference is now I know how to manage it all. I can't make it go away. My heart is beating fast, and I keep coming back to this thinking, *"I can't believe I am writing this."*

I lay in bed every night when I was little in fear or in pain. My earaches were so bad I thought I was dying. My mom would gently lay my head down and put sweet oil in them each time.

Then she would take me to the doctor where I would sit for hours to get medicine. The doctors would always make comments about the number of scars I had on my eardrums. That goes all the way back to the mice in my crib.

Yes, it's very real. I was born in North Carolina. We lived there until I was two years old. My parents would tell me stories of how when they would wake up in the middle of the night or in the morning, there would be mice in my bed--all over me. It took me years to shake that story.

I was in and out of the doctor until I was 4 years old-- underweight and sick. I could not drink regular milk. I weighed a whole 13 pounds until I was 4 years old. My mom says one day it all turned around. I started to gain weight and look healthy. I believe I am paying for that now. I have battled my weight my whole life—gaining it unconsciously so men would not be attracted to me physically but instead to my mind and my energy.

I sure did succeed. My brain is a masterpiece and I am grateful for it every day. I am beautiful and have accepted my beauty on all levels. However, like lots of people, I'm trying to get the last 60 pounds off.

We moved when I was 2 years old to a small town in Missouri. We lived in a trailer court that flooded often. My uncle would bring his boat in to pull us out every time it flooded. The waters were so deep and dirty we could not get in it. We would all be piled up in this little boat where we were taken out a few people at a time. At the entrance I remember volunteers always had hot chocolate and warm biscuits waiting for us to make us feel safe and warm.

So many things happened in the trailer court. That is where my first encounter of sexual abuse occurred. I will not give you details but as little girl going through that, I can tell you I felt trapped, scared, and lonely. I was very confused and did not know how to make it stop. My parents were always working like most of the other parents I knew.

When my parents were home, our house was full of stress and anger. We knew when my dad pulled up, the house should be spotless. If it was not, we paid for it. My mom tried so hard to take care of us. I don't remember her yelling. She was always trying to keep us together. She was so wrapped up in surviving. I could always see the unhappiness in her face.

She wanted it to be different. She just did not know how. She had been with my dad since she was 13 years old. My dad was a good man inside, but he never worked out the stuff in his own head and was barely able to function and know what to do. He would hit every defense possible. He always seemed to be in his Circle of Crazy.

Worrying about bills, money, and I am sure things I don't even understand, he was constantly fighting with my brothers. I know they always felt under attack. I know you might be thinking, "who did this little girl have to help her," and the answer is no one. I wanted so bad to protect my little sister and brother that I just dealt with what I had to. We eventually moved from that place and into a place that would change the course of my life even more. I wish I could tell you things got better but I cannot.

We moved into a subdivision that was mainly trailers. Every road was a dirt road. We lived on 5 acres in the same trailer. My parents now had farther to drive for work and were gone even longer hours.

I can easily skip this section. As I write this, I am not sure where to go next. So, I am just going to write. There was so much abuse in these years that I look back now and wonder how can any child encounter so much pain? My dad was constantly in his mess. When he would come home from having a bad day, he took it out on us. I was scared that if there was one piece of paper on the floor, we would pretty much get beaten. One day he came home to laundry being in baskets. That was something we should never do. His response was to throw every piece of clothing out the back door. If that weren't bad enough, he started throwing things on the floor breaking vases and dishes telling us that we did not take care of anything. It got worse, but I will stop there.

Today, I have a good relationship with my dad. I know he had his own Circle of Crazy. Those behaviors were not ok. I did not choose to live there. It is what was dealt to me as a child.

In addition to all of that happening at home, I would go to school where I was being bullied, made fun of, called names, and felt like I was living on the outside. I was not a shy girl, but I kept to myself. I tried to stand up for myself in school and sometimes made it worse. My seventh-grade year was the worst. I had already experienced a lot of sexual trauma, and it just kept coming. I was in seventh grade trying to find my place in the world and one guy made me feel very special. He was one grade older than me.

Little did I know there was more to come. We started hanging out, and one day everything changed. I found myself trapped in his room being raped. He would apologize, make me feel special, and do it all over again. One day led to many days of being locked scared in his room where I was raped over and over. How did I get there you might be asking, it's another story for another day.

It is hard to give you, the reader, every detail of how my life rolled out. I was scared and my parents were in their own world and had no clue what I was going through. By the time I was a freshman in high school, I had already been abused sexually by 5 different people.

I filled my time with friends who were older than me. Some were great for me and some were not. I had two brother figures in my life who protected me from so many things. We were so close. They made me feel like I had people—my people. We hung out day after day. They were my best friends and two people I give credit for saving my life on so many levels. They may not know it until they read this book. They knew nothing of what I experienced in my life. They did know my dad well, and they wanted to protect me. They were always there for me and never hurt me.

Sure, there were a few times we had crushes on each other, but it was always just a crush. I had a few close friends that seemed to come and go. Two girls were with me through much of my life. They never knew anything I had experienced other than with my dad. I got mixed up with some really wrong crowds and always found my way out. I thank God that I did. Sometimes I can't believe I am still here when others are not.

I have seen the trauma losing people. Two friends died in car accidents, my cousin was killed at 15 by a drunk driver, and my grandpa died from cancer just when I started to get to know him. I took care of him. I was the only one he would allow to change his bandages. I was not there the day he died. I will always remember him sitting at the kitchen table just being himself. He never hurt me and loved me without ever saying it. I lost my favorite uncle 12 years ago to cancer. He was another man who loved me and never hurt me. His daughter was the one who was killed by a drunk driver at 15.

We didn't have running water a lot of the time and our electric was always being shut off. We were just surviving. My parents bounced checks to feed us. Holidays were always a giant battle, especially Christmas. My parents never had the money to buy us things and it always ended in big fights. My parents were always fighting. My mom was always trying to get away.

I was always the one getting in the middle of the fights. I was the one that could get my dad calmed down, I still am! I had my dad taken to jail one crazy evening or at least that's what he remembers, and he has never forgiven me for that. I said this earlier, but my dad is a good person. He has changed. He still has his days. I had to come to grips with the fact that he is who he is, and I can never change that.

I have dealt with pain and chaos my whole life. I was the girl that got in the middle of the fights happening at home trying to stop them. I begged my mom to divorce my dad. When she tried, his anger pulled her back in.

There were some good things too. I have always had good people in my life who would try to help me. They knew I had something going on, but they never knew the extent. I remember one of my neighbors taking me to church. Back then it was called Awana.

We went every Wednesday night. My mom loved to go to church but my dad never did. Unfortunately, my mom was always caught up in his stuff, and she never fully engaged in going like she wanted. My grandma and our neighbor took me often. It was my safe place where no one could hurt me. I believe today that my neighbor saved my life. She knows nothing of what I experienced growing up, and yet, she influenced me in a way that helped me move forward knowing that God had me.

When I was 16 years old, I was driving to the gas station that was 2 miles from our house. I was driving with 5 other people in the car: my best friend, my sister, a neighbor girl whom we were watching, and my best friend's little boy.

We were heading down to get a soda and just being kids. We had noticed these very cute guys in the parking lot. As young girls do, we were acting silly. I got behind the wheel to drive away with these 5 people in the car. I pulled out on the road, looked out my window, and whistled to get these boys' attention. They started yelling back. My sister, best friend, and I were very distracted. I started to make a left-hand turn--only I never stopped to look. That's the last thing I remember. We were hit by a one-ton dually truck on its way to rescue a horse. Our car was mangled. The five of us in the car were barely alive.

Fire trucks, police, and people were surrounding us. My parents came to the scene in a panic. That's what I was told. Bodies being pulled from the car and loaded into the ambulance. My best friend was airlifted because she was barely alive. All of us spent days in the hospital. After all of that, the only thing I have held onto was a story my parents told me of a pastor who prayed over the car and put on my seatbelt. To this day I have no idea why he put my seatbelt on, but his prayer must have saved our lives.

Can you imagine the weight I was carrying at 16 years old?

From abuse to almost killing everyone in that car. I knew that I did not kill everyone in that car but, man, it took some time to heal. I did not want to drive a lot of places. I was scared for people to be in my car for years to come. Early in our marriage, my husband would have to take off work to take our kids to the doctor. One thing was linked to the next. One event affected another.

I have had many people in my life that have worked side-by-side with me, helping me to reach many levels in my life and some have been life-changing for me. I could write a book just on the impact people have had on my life. One day, I might do just that, but today I want to tell you about one man that truly helped me see what I was capable of. He helped me pull all this craziness to the surface and begin to let it go and live. By the time I met him, I had already had kids and had been married for 7 years to a wonderful man who I am still head-over-heels for today.

One day I flipped on the TV and heard a man talking about family and relationships. I felt like he was speaking right to me. I had a feeling inside of me that said pick up the phone call him. I did just that. This man went on to mentor, coach, and support me for years to come. He is responsible for mending my heart and opening it up to a world full of possibility. He changed my life.

The little girl that was inside of me trying to keep everything from coming to the surface had now shared her story with a single man. From there he led me on a journey to de-clutter my mind and my heart! I decided I wanted to 10X my Inner Rockstar. For the first time I felt I had a real chance to take my life to another level. He helped me work through all the stories, events, and circumstances that were keeping me from being me.

One day as we were going into a coaching session, I was shaking, nervous, not sure what to expect. I had a thought that would repeat in my brain over and over *"he will never know certain things about me because he would look at me as if I was the dirtiest person ever. Don't say anything. Don't say anything."* He began to talk with me and within minutes I broke down. I was in tears, scared, and worried that my life would change forever.

Within seconds I told him details I promised I would never share. At that time all I had was negative thoughts hidden by a positive attitude. I could not hold it in. It had to come out. He looked at me and said, "I am so proud of you. I am here and will not leave you." I felt right then the weight I had been carrying for so long had been lifted. I drove home that day in tears thinking, *"What did I just do?"*

My head and my heart did not know how to feel. I wanted him to see me for me and not all that other stuff.

I believe in my heart that's why it has taken me so long to write this book. I want the world to see me--not the stuff I have been through. Months into working with him I was changed. I felt like I had not just hope but peace. So much so that one day I had to have a talk with my husband. I was scared and shaking. Why? Because my husband never knew anything about my childhood. He had heard stories and knew there was stuff but never knew details. He was one more person that I wanted to see me for me and not for the stuff I went through.

We were cleaning out back yard one day and I looked at him and said, "I need to tell you something." I walked over, looked in his eyes, broke down, and let it out. He looked back at me and said these exact words, "I love you more now than ever, and now I know why you are the way you are." LIFE CHANGING! He has never stopped loving me. In fact, he said I will never stop you from being you and impacting people. He has made more sacrifices for me and the people I serve than you could ever imagine.

I always knew I was meant for more and no one could take that from me. Even when I took the world on my shoulders.

What I know now is I am not broken; shit happened. It did not happen because of me or to me; it just happened. It was not a personal attack, and I did not cause any of it. I don't like any of it, but I am thankful for the chaos I have had in my life. Storms never stop coming. We have to learn to dance in the rain.

Often, people ask me how I got out ok. My answer is God, faith, determination, people, my gifts, the desire to change lives, my family, the plan that was created for me.

Why me? I don't know. Why YOU? I don't know. But why keep asking? Pain is pain. We will always experience some level of it at different times in our lives. Let's just keep paddling 10 times harder, get rid of the stories in our heads, and be the people we were created to be. We have all been through shit. We can't change that. Embrace it.

I absolutely love my life. I have been married for 19 years and have four amazing children. I have not even begun to tell you about my life after 18, but I will tell you it is full of more stories, failures, and lots of success. I have been working to 10X my Inner Rockstar for years. The real start to that was one weekend at a seminar where I thought I was perfect. I thought I had nothing to work on and I was proven wrong. I was a real mess and that weekend literally changed my life.

I found myself with many walls trying to hide my hurt. One single hour showed me a completely different side. I was surrounded by people working through an exercise one person at a time. It came to my turn, and I just would not let go. The leader looked right into my eyes and said, "forget about her. Let's take a break." I was crushed. I thought I was messed up. I was left out. That feeling got stronger after the break when the afternoon went on. I still just did not want to let go.

All of the sudden the leader called me to the middle of the room, had everyone surround me, and put their hands on me. He pulled every little thing out of me that needed to come out. I will never forget what he did for me. I learned they did not forget. They cared and wanted to help. I just had to let go and let them.

I am a freaking Rockstar and no one, not even my past, can take that away from me. I won't allow it. Today, I allow emotions in. I take time to process. I pay attention. I invite the chaos so I can crush it. I am who I am.

I know that you can do this. You can be the Rockstar you were created to be no matter what your life has thrown at you no matter what has happened in the past. You are who you are, and your story is your story. I know it's not easy, but I wake up every day remembering that I was created to be awesome, and I keep moving. I will not let these things win. I play to win. I want to work every day at 10Xing my Inner Rockstar for my family and for you. I have taken this journey myself and I know firsthand it is not easy-- especially if you have family and people around you that depend on you.

It's hard, but it's a must. I am here for you every step of the way and will pray that you 10X Your Inner Rockstar. Your story does not have to be like mine. You could have had a very simple life and still feel like something deep in you is not being fulfilled. No matter what your reason, you are here to be the person you were created to be and to 10X Your Inner Rockstar.

Rockstar Connection:

1. What is your story? Write bullets points of your life and how they might have affected your life?
2. Has your story held you back or pushed you forward?
3. How can your story encourage, inspire, and change lives of people around you?

JAM SESSION 3

Ambush Of Thoughts And Emotions

Are Emotions/Thoughts Keeping You "Stuck" in Your Journey to Become a Rockstar?

Often, we lose ourselves because we are overwhelmed by life's events - childhood traumas, circumstances, and life's happenings around us. Our thoughts and emotions affect our perception.

In fact, did you know that the thoughts in your brain are hundreds of years old? Your brain is like one big emotional warehouse housing the beliefs and perceptions of the most influential people in your life. Your influences can be good or bad. Did you know that most ideas are not original thoughts? Most people want to claim their ideas and thoughts as brand new.

There are between 25,000 and 50,000 thoughts that enter your brain daily coming from TV, music, road signs, kids, spouses, school, work, teams, books, and so on.

Often, the people who join my program are overwhelmed by the chaos in their minds. They are confused and have no idea of how to stop the craziness that has taken over their lives. Making good, rational decisions has become very difficult for them. My approach for almost any client is to: calm the chaos, find the patterns, declutter the mind, and start the healing process. It doesn't matter who you are or what you are dealing with, there are no shortcuts. You must first learn how to deal with your emotions and feelings in a healthy way. Then, you can move confidently ahead toward success.

Quick Action Step

Grab a piece of paper and write down your age. Now multiply that by 365. What does that equal? Multiply that by 30,000 thoughts that you could have in ONE day. How many thoughts have you had since the beginning of your life? (Now, I would like to make a point for all my analytical people. You did not have 30,000 thoughts as a newborn. But I think you get the point!) Go ahead and grab your calculator. What does that number look like? How does it make you feel?

I can tell you that when I did the math, I was shocked. If you have millions of thoughts consuming your brain power, it is easy to understand why it is so hard to do the right thing or even finish just a few tasks. Your brain is in a constantly overloaded state. With thousands of thoughts coming in daily, how do you filter them or make the right decisions?

Now, consider that your overloaded brain may be sitting on old, distorted beliefs that aren't even yours. You cannot possibly take the right action or even make the right decisions most of the time.

With millions of thoughts zipping from synapse to synapse inside your head, how do you process your thoughts, let alone break patterns and cycles?

Reading *The Power of Habit* by Charles Duhigg was an intriguing and scary experience for me. It confirmed my belief that the world and the people around us are affecting our minds. The real question is how do we take everything in and do something constructive with it?

I have gained a lifetime of experience serving people. As I sat down with literally hundreds of people – couples, children, and leaders – I saw patterns and cycles unfold. I have seen people live their lives trying to figure out why they can't break out of old patterns, habits, and cycles.

People believe that they are destined to fail and that they must be depressed. This happens in people healthy or unhealthy. Life consists of cycles and patterns. Deep inside those patterns and habits are blind spots – blind spots that could be affecting your life. Often, we don't know what we don't know because we don't know that we don't know it. Life happens around us and forces us to feel things internally causing us to act out. You are attracting things and people to your life based on how you feel on the inside.

These emotions could be fear, guilt, anger, shame, loneliness, worry, and stress. When those emotions hit, we act out in ways that affect our lives. When we are stressed, we can play victim, go into fight or flight, use painkillers, or even hit defense mechanisms. What does that mean for you?

In summary, we all have junk in our heads, and we are all screwed up trying to figure this world out. That will never stop. Your brain and your heart are trying hard to keep up. It is important to understand that to 10X Your Inner

Rockstar will require you to first discover YOU, declutter your brain, and fuel your life.

Rockstar Connection:

1. What emotions seem to give you the most trouble (you are looking for a pattern) and might be a clue to what is standing in your way of becoming the Rockstar you are created to be (anger, frustration, anxiety, fear, etc.)?
2. Just because thoughts pop in your mind does NOT mean they are true.

   What stories do you tell yourself?
   Common examples are:
   - I don't have many friends.
   - I am broke.
   - I will never get out of debt.

   What are the stories you were told growing up?
   Common examples are:
   - Money does not grow on trees.
   - You will never be a professional hockey player (singer, actor, etc.)

3. Do you spend time or expend energy worrying about those thoughts that are lies (which will move you further away from your goal of becoming a Rockstar)?
4. What thoughts or emotions fuel you and give you a sense of energy and well-being?

JAM SESSION 4

Rule Your Emotions

Do you understand what emotions really are? How can you use them effectively? What is the purpose of emotions? What do they mean? How can they be controlled?

It's sunny one minute and the next minute we have dark clouds overhead. That is kind of how life is, right? One of my favorite sayings reminds me of the teachings of the great Wayne Dyer: *Storms never stop coming. You must learn to dance in the rain.*

Storms are a part of life. They help us to develop character. They give us growth experiences. They give us meaning. They give us heart and empathy. They give us a variety of life experiences. But what really matters most is how we deal with the storms of life. You must never forget that it's not about what has happened or is happening to you. It is your reaction to it that determines your result. You can't live according to how you feel and 10X Your Inner Rockstar.

Our emotions are fickle, they can change very fast. You feel great this minute and the next you feel horrible. You may go to bed motivated but wake up not so excited. You simply don't feel like getting out of bed. Are you going to stay in bed all day? No, you have got to push yourself out of that bed. We must be the master of our emotions.

My childhood was not the greatest. That may be your story, too. I believed that I was emotional because I overheard

51

people in my family saying, "Leisa is an emotional child."
What did that mean really? I thought there must be
something wrong with me as I tried to process everything
from a child's perspective. Those same childhood
experiences deeply impacted my perception as an adult
without my even realizing it. My adult perception was
terribly distorted, since I was still looking at many of life's
experiences through the eyes of a child. It took me many
years to understand how my early childhood experiences
have profoundly affected many of my decisions and actions
later in life.

Now I understand emotions are a necessary part of life and
they provide invaluable opportunities to learn and grow. My
emotions were there for a reason just like yours are.
However, we must learn how to manage them in a healthy
way. Emotions and experiences help us navigate through
the storms of life that come at us each day. Emotions will
always be with us. How we control them determines our
results. When you learn to rule your emotions, you will see
having emotions as a blessing. Now is the time to stop
invalidating your emotions, and instead, use them to live an
abundant and full life.

Rockstar Connection:

1. What do you want in life?
2. Why does your emotional health matter?
3. Do your emotions control you or do you control your
   emotions?
4. Do you feel like storms are always coming at you?
5. Do you let your emotions drive you toward action or
   inaction?

JAM SESSION 5

How you perceive today's experiences directly correlates with the experiences that you had before the age of 18. Most of your belief system developed between the ages of five and 10. Believe it or not, those years have the greatest impact on your life. The environment, people, and emotions of your childhood strongly influence the beliefs you have today. During those years, the "why you do what you do" develops. Think about who was in your life and how they played a role.

What were their beliefs? Did you internalize them? Who influenced your influencers? Your story came from another story that came from another story. Years of beliefs and perceptions have been passed down from generation to generation. Your belief system was not fed by one person but by many. As a result, most people are not sure what they stand for, and unfortunately, live a life of incongruence.

In other words, they live a life marked by confusion as they try to dig deep into their own meaning and purpose on this earth. What they are seeking is to know their true self without the noise of so many others' beliefs.

Most people cannot figure this out on their own. They need a coach who is trained specifically in this area to help them understand this at its core. Helping people find their Inner Rockstar is what I have done for many years now.

Who is in Your Clubhouse?

Who is in your clubhouse? These are the people we surround ourselves with, the people we spend time with and talk to regularly – think friends, family, and coworkers. Your clubhouse of friends is either serving you or taking away from you. Their influence is either positive or negative and can impact why you do what you do.

We actively seek to be accepted for who we are. We like to think for ourselves and create our own way of doing things, but the truth is that we learn most or a large portion of who we are from the people in our clubhouse or the people who have been part of our lives from the beginning. Sometimes the people in your clubhouse are referred to as your reference group. Many of the things we come to see as our way of doing things started becoming a part of us even before we said our very first words on earth.

The people in your life have so much influence over you that without realizing it you conform to it.

Brian Tracy stated that if a person went for a training and learned new skills and ways of doing things and was excited about applying the new skills in his life, inevitably he would revert to his old self in a matter of few weeks after returning to his reference group.

Simply put, no change sticks if you remain in your reference group unless the change happens to the whole group. Others have said we are the average of the five people closest to us.

Napoleon Hill said you end up having the same level of success as those in the mastermind or group of success-minded people that you meet or work with on a regular basis. He said no great power or success is possible without the mastermind.

When you started to read this book, you might have felt like you were at an emotional low. If I asked you on a scale from 1 to 10 how you felt inside right now, what would your answer be? Did you realize if you feel like a 6, you attract people who also feel like a 6? As you grow, your number will rise, and you will begin to move away from the group that you had in your life before.

Most people will ask, "Is this ok? Why do I feel this way? I don't want to turn my back on anyone." It's a normal feeling. If this begins to happen, you know that you are moving closer to 10Xing Your Inner Rockstar.

> If you go to www.10xYourInnerRockstar.com,we have communication resources to help you.

I have heard others in my profession say that people have control over their own decisions. I do not totally agree with this statement. Sometimes the hand you were dealt was not fair. You did not ask to be placed in a specific home or given certain negative influences.

However, it is important that you do not let your negative circumstances become a crutch or an excuse to hold you back. You must learn to embrace and understand that the circumstances in your life made you who you are. They built your character whether good or bad. But the good news is that you have the final say in your life—you get to choose how you react to your specific situation.

Our minds get overloaded with others' opinions and information in general. We are literally DROWNING in it. Do you ever feel like you get lost in trying to figure everything out? When you have to make a decision, do you feel like you must run it by 6 people first hoping that they will help you? Does it help? Usually, it makes things worse. All of those opinions make you feel like you are living in limbo and confused. All of that information usually does not help you move forward.

Think of this, if you are getting opinions from other people who are in their Circle of Crazy and wrapped up in their challenges, you are getting opinions based on their distorted perception and not based on a neutral, unbiased one. There are millions of people out there that offer great advice and can be a real benefit to you. But how do you find them or figure out if your friends are affecting your life in a negative or positive way?

If you really want to 10X Your Inner Rockstar, then take a really hard look at who is in your clubhouse or is part of your reference group. If you are ready to move forward, here is how to start. Look at your core group.

Ask yourself these questions:

- Do they complain 70% of the time?
- Do they always seem to be in a funk?
- Are they heavily opinionated without your asking for advice?
- Do you have someone in your life that keeps you from moving forward?
- Do you have someone who takes advantage of you?
- Do you cringe when the phone rings and it's them?
- Do they complain on Facebook nonstop?

If you answered yes to any of those questions, then you have people surrounding that are not helping you 10X Your Inner Rockstar.

It is time to go back to that childhood clubhouse and decide who will be in it with you. It is time to stop hiding and use the strength God gave you to choose what is best for you. Stand on your own two feet and say, "I do not need to defend my actions and I will decide what I need." You have a voice. No more invalidating your feelings or questioning yourself and your environment.

Rockstar Connection:

1. Think back to the formative years of your childhood. Can you identify any beliefs or perceptions that you accepted as part of your persona without really evaluating whether they were true or not?
2. Are those beliefs holding you back from achieving your full potential or living the life you desire for yourself or loved ones?

3. If you find yourself reacting to certain situations in a negative way, stop and take note. Feel the emotion and try to figure out where it is coming from. You may even want to keep a journal of emotions if necessary. This is a great way to discover emotional patterns and triggers. For example, you may become upset and uncomfortable when someone raises his or her voice in a certain way because it triggers painful childhood memories.
4. Who is in your clubhouse and how are they affecting you today?

JAM SESSION 6

How the Circle of Crazy Can Block Your Path to Becoming a Rockstar

Are emotions good or bad? Society has given a negative connotation to having emotions, but emotions are necessary. I want you to embrace your emotions, take control of them, think clearly, and take your life to a new level. Emotions are neither good nor bad. Emotions cause reactions or actions. You get to decide how you want to utilize the emotions you have. My goal in this book is to help you learn to dance in the rain, gain control of your emotional roller coaster, and confidently overcome one obstacle at a time.

It is often said that your life is a journey. However, I think of it as more of a roller coaster and obstacle course. You jump one hurdle, only to find another one is right around the corner. A journey sounds so relaxing, inviting, and peaceful. Can we agree that life is just not like that most of the time? We can plan our hearts out, but something unexpected is bound to happen. For example, you are on your way to a business meeting that you think will lead to your dream job. You have worked your whole life to get to this point, but your child spikes a fever at the last minute. You have no one to watch him.

Suddenly, you are in panic mode. What do you do? How do you handle it?

59

Do you seek alcohol or meds to calm you down? Do you act out of frustration and find yourself yelling only to feel guilty about it later? Or are you able to calmly think through the situation and find a solution?

Have you ever felt like you were about to explode? Or have you ever felt lonely, worried, sad, and/or stressed? Once one or more of these emotions come to the surface, do you find yourself shutting down, grabbing a drink, eating, taking medication, self-sabotaging, or simply just being the nice guy or gal to smooth things over? That, my friends, is the Circle of Crazy. Have you ever been there? Unless you are Mother Teresa, I am sure that you have. You might even find yourself in the Circle of Crazy up to five times a day or more.

This can lead to thought distortions: magnifying the situation, foretelling a doomsday future, or even "shoulding" on yourself. "Shoulding" on yourself refers to using words such as "should," "need to," "ought to," or "must" in order to motivate yourself. But instead, it leads to feelings of guilt when you fail to follow through (or anger and resentment when someone else does not follow through).

At any point on a given day, we can be sucked into the Circle of Crazy. Some may even live there on a permanent basis! Being stressed, feeling guilty or fearful, and/or constant worry can take over our lives. When we feel any of these emotions, we can act out in many destructive ways. We may play the victim and blame others for what is happening or not happening in our lives. We may make excuses and use the words we all know so well, "I can't."

Our bodies go into "fight or flight" mode and everything and everyone that comes at us will be perceived negatively. We may use painkillers or other prescription drugs, hide on social media, watch TV, overeat, escape with porn, or drink ourselves to a better weekend.

Or we may use one of the common defense mechanisms, such as shutting down, staying quiet, refusing to participate, keeping others from winning, self-sabotaging, or intentionally creating problems.

How do you handle your emotions? Do you spiral from one emotion to another? Do you fly right into the Circle of Crazy? Keep in mind that when you or others are acting out of their Circle of Crazy, you also affect everyone else you are around – especially children.

What I will tell you is whether you have suffered from deep childhood wounds, the loss of a child, divorce, abuse, rape, sexual abuse, mental or physical abuse, you should seek professional help and guidance. It is important to understand where your emotions come from and what triggers them. When under pressure, old hurts come to the surface. And without realizing it, you begin reacting to them in a way you swore you would never do.

Everything that we have experienced in life, good or bad, has an impact on us and explains WHY we do what we do. The point is to identify your triggers and make sure that you set healthy boundaries in your relationships.

It is important to avoid triggering the emotions that take you into the Circle of Crazy and develop strategies to keep you out of it.

Rockstar Connection:

1. What coping mechanisms do you most often use? What leads you to use those coping mechanisms?
2. What are some strategies that you could implement to keep from entering the Circle of Crazy in the first place and help you reach your goals?
3. How many times do you use the word "should" in a typical day? "Should" often brings guilt and unproductive emotions to your psyche. Try eliminating the word from your vocabulary altogether and replace it with "can" or "will" or "get to" or some other more specific term.

JAM SESSION 7

Emotional Intelligence is in part the perception, control, and evaluation of your emotions and the emotions of others. With high emotional intelligence, you can recognize, control, and express your emotions to weather life's storms effectively and learn from them. You can build character through emotion and experience.

How do you deal with your emotions? Do you allow emotional triggers to take you back to familiar and comfortable patterns? Or do you choose to grow in character through challenging times?

Imagine two people faced with the same problem. One person takes full responsibility and uses the situation to grow. He strives to be aware of his own emotions, feelings, and blind spots.

This is an example of someone with a high level of emotional intelligence. The other person displays low emotional intelligence by playing the victim, lacking awareness of his emotions, and blaming others for the situation. Each person will experience very different results because of the choices made, even though they were faced with the same situation.

Developing emotional intelligence starts with your ability to identify and manage your emotions in a productive way. Increased emotional intelligence can be learned if you are open to the process.

63

The first step to developing emotional intelligence is assessing your emotional state. If you feel guilt, anger, fear, loneliness, shame or worry, you may be in the Circle of Crazy. Remember, when you're in the Circle of Crazy, your emotions are like an out-of-control roller coaster and you may not be able to see a way out.

In addition to escalating negative feelings, being in the Circle of Crazy makes it extremely hard to see things as they really are. When your emotions cycle over and over, you stay in the Circle of Crazy. You may be hitting walls, using defense mechanisms, and/or even abusing painkillers. The Circle of Crazy affects all areas of your life. But once you learn how to recognize this destructive pattern, you're one step closer to being able to manage your emotions successfully.

Sometimes it takes hitting rock bottom or simply experiencing a crisis for some people to have an awakening. That's when they realize something must change. It is hard for most people to recognize that their reality is based on perceptions not facts.

Most people believe that when their emotional intelligence is raised, they will never be angry, frustrated, or upset again. This simply is not true. Negative emotions are a part of life. But will you use them for action or reaction, comfort or growth, certainty or uncertainty? It is common and natural for most people to go back to the comfortable and familiar patterns during an emotional moment or decision.

It is easy to do. You know what your familiar patterns taste, smell, look, and feel like. There are no guessing games.

There is a comfort in certainty. You have been there before, but the fear and triggers that you developed to protect yourself may keep you from experiencing life fully.

Triggers bring up familiar emotions stored in your brain and nerve system. You unconsciously file experiences in your brain that affect your everyday life. Uncertainty is, just that—uncertain and scary and uncomfortable. You are sailing into unknown and unchartered waters.

Most people file negative emotions and triggers, instead of positive ones. It is how the human brain is wired. That means many of the good things and experiences in life get covered up. To retrain your brain—to file and see the good—means you need to file moments of strength and accomplishment. Visualize them, feel them, and file them accordingly. Those are the emotions you want to pull out when it is time to jump out of your comfort zone into unfamiliar waters. Those energized and empowered feelings will carry you more than you know when facing sudden changes or challenging situations.

We will dive deeper into self-awareness as the cornerstone of emotional intelligence in an upcoming Jam Session.

"All learning has an emotional base." – Plato

Rockstar Connection:

1. What are some moments of strength and accomplishment in your life? Feel them and visualize them so that you can learn to carry them with you in a positive way as you move toward your aspirations.

2. Think back on major decisions you have made in your life. How many of your decisions were made primarily out of emotion? Make a habit of delaying a decision if you are in a high emotional state.
3. When you get into your Circle of Crazy, what are 3 action steps to help you get out of it?

JAM SESSION 8

Understanding the Emotional Brain

Your brain is emotional. I have said this a few times in this book. You were created to have emotions. Often, I hear people tell stories of pushing emotions away and down because of limited beliefs or not knowing how to deal with what comes to the surface. Who wants to deal with all of those feelings? Sometimes it just seems easier to be numb. Some people might be overly emotional because they never learned to manage emotions or figure out how to use emotions in a positive way. I can't emphasize this enough – this happens to all of us. One thing I hope you are learning is that I don't want you to ignore what comes up. It is information for the journey you are on. Pay attention to your body and what you need. Read this breakdown of emotions below. Take note of what season you are in and what you need to do to Take Action Fearlessly and 10X Your Inner Rockstar.

⇨ Recognizing Emotions

You must be able to recognize emotions accurately. This is not always an easy task. Most people have built emotional walls because of their life experiences.

Perceiving emotion must be from a non-judgmental place outside of your Circle of Crazy. The way you perceive life, events, and circumstances is the foundation of how you will live your life.

⇨ Your Triggered Emotions

You must understand where your emotions come from. Everything you have filed away in your subconscious brain is tied to an emotion that you have felt in the past. Most often, it is an emotion that has caused stress to your body, good or bad. For example, you will remember a car accident because it caused stress to your body, but you may not remember what you had for dinner a few days ago. Dinner most likely did not cause good or bad stress unless it was a special occasion or you had an intense argument.

When emotion strikes in a chaotic situation, you are often triggered by an emotion that has been filed away. Your body remembers that emotion and it easily finds its way back to you like a familiar friend. You may think that emotion is your reality, but it's just a perception based on a familiar experience of those feelings. So, you must learn to reason with your emotions and not allow them to play tricks on you by distorting your thoughts.

⇨ Understanding Emotions

Emotions have a variety of meanings. Understand that emotions cannot attack you personally. They are only feelings that you have assigned a meaning. You may be angry and come off to someone else as rude. But what does that emotion mean and what triggered it? Or maybe you wonder why someone is taking things so personally.

The answers are often not so easy to come by. It takes time and effort to uncover why people behave as they do. For example, a deep-seated fear may explain why someone is defensive or is lashing out at you. We do not know what caused them to be in their Circle of Crazy. While it is always helpful to try to understand their journey, it is important that you work on understanding your emotions first.

⇨ **Managing Emotions**

This seems to be the hardest part of all for most people. Life just does not stop. It is hard to rein it in and process the 25,000 – 50,000 thoughts and decisions that come at us each day. But believe it or not, this is a skill that can be taught in a few simple steps.

The ability to manage emotions effectively is a crucial part of emotional intelligence. Regulating emotions, acting appropriately, and responding to the emotions of others are all important aspects of emotional management. Your nerve system will respond to the emotions you are feeling and affect your body in a negative or positive way. Managing your emotions is not just important for communicating with others but for your overall health.

What you think about and feel is what you get.

I have seen clients come into my office completely stressed out. As a result, they may be dealing with high blood pressure, depression, anxiety, or other medical issues.

The default solution of society is to put these people on blood pressure medication, antidepressants, or long-term counseling programs. I want to stop for a minute to tell you that I am not anti-medicine. Medicine has its place in society. I do not put people on medicine or take them off, but I will support their journey moving forward with or without it. Medicine provides a pattern interrupt in your nerve system that will slow your thoughts, brain, and body down. Sometimes that could cause a negative reaction, but sometimes it's needed for people who can't find another option.

I do not recommend you run right out and get on medication; however, you need to find what works for you, so you aren't living an unfulfilled life. Medicine will not solve your problems. When dealing with emotions, it only provides a temporary solution and may only mask the cause of the problems. It is likely your problems will come back.

Pattern interrupts occur with many other resources such as chiropractic care, natural paths, music, walking, hypnosis, so many other things. You will notice I said music. YES! Music can provide the same effects as medicine in some people depending on what the problem is. It is important to understand how your brain works, who you are, and what you SPECIFICALLY need--not what others say you need.

The key is that if you are thinking negatively, feeling stressed, living in your Circle of Crazy, repeating patterns, feeling broken, then you are living in the logic side of your brain. Slowing it down is necessary but not enough. You need to do something to engage the creative side. That is how you break the cycle and move forward.

Your logic brain is needed but can take over your life. Your creative brain needs to come out and play. You need to have both sides of your brain working congruently. When people are suicidal, it's because they are consumed with negative thoughts or negative people. Their brain is spiraling out of control. They are living in the logic side and cannot control it. They are on information overload with no end in sight.

Encouragement and love go along way and may provide a pattern interrupt, but most friends and family don't know how to intervene effectively. That is why outside resources work.

One of my clients had deep pain buried inside of her that she refused to acknowledge. She did everything to stop it from coming to the surface. She drank, smoked, and partied hard. She used sex to shut down. Cancer was ravaging her body. She was in and out of the hospital with treatment after treatment. She finally reached a point in her life where she knew change had to happen.

She decided to share her story with me. She told me about how she was physically and sexually abused. When she told me that her cancer was in her uterus, I knew that it was very possible that the stress that she had experienced from her abuse was showing up in her body because she had not dealt with her emotions in a healthy way. I know that this story may blow your mind, but people often have physical ailments due to emotional stress.

What you need to know is that I have discovered a way to dig out what is causing your stress. The process helps to uncover the person you were created to be, teach you how to manage your emotions long-term, and get rid of this stuff forever, so it NEVER takes over your body! This is the most invigorating part of my career in serving and coaching others.

My program is based around teaching people how to become independent. I have proven tools that will help you break out of self-limiting patterns and develop your emotional intelligence to levels you have never seen before. What I get to experience every day is people believing what is possible for them.

The client I mentioned above first started believing it was possible to heal because I listened to her. I heard her struggles and I told her to stop taking action for the sake of just taking action. I knew that she had dealt with major pain and suffering in her life like so many others. People are often only willing to share about 2% of what is going on in their lives. Why? Because people are not very good listeners. You may be like 70% of the world who spend most of their time in conversations talking and focusing on themselves. This woman had real hurts and real problems. She needed someone to listen and care. She started to retrain her brain, discover herself, declutter her brain, and finally take the "right" action. Not only did she heal emotionally, but when she went back to the doctor her cancer was miraculously gone!

While you may not believe that her emotional healing was tied to her physical healing, there is no doubt in my mind that it had a significant impact. She is now living the life she was created to live. She stopped attracting the wrong and started believing she was worth the right. In summary, it is important to understand how negative emotions impact your body, your mind, your heart, and your soul. All are connected and should be approached in a holistic matter.

If you do not learn to recognize, manage, and use your emotions in a healthy manner, you could be hurting your health, body, and relationships. Decide right now that you are not going to hide or ignore your emotions anymore and that you are going to use them for good.

Rockstar Connection:

1. Are you playing to win or are you playing NOT to lose? Are you even on the field?
2. Do you really believe that you can achieve the desires of your heart?
3. Are you holding on to stress, un-forgiveness, or fears that may be holding you back emotionally or physically? For example, do you have high blood pressure, grind your teeth, deal with weight issues, or have chronic tight muscles? Check out the next Jam Session and highlight areas that might be of concern.

JAM SESSION 9

The Effects of Negative Emotions on Your Body

I have dedicated an entire chapter on how your emotions could be affecting your body. This is so important to understand as your body is the only vessel you have. If you are not managing your emotions, your body will find a way to deal with those emotions and that could be in a negative way.

You could be dealing with major illness or minor aches and pains. I believe that is your body's way of dealing with what you won't. I hope you have read my story and if you have not, go back and witness the level of emotion and chaos I have been through. I did not know that I had things to deal with.

All I knew was I just wanted to hide it until one day I woke up and realized I was overweight, yelling at my kids, and living in a place I did not want to be. I was not truly happy with who I was and worked hard to understand WHY I had to experience all the things in life. I was releasing negative stress into my body and carrying it in a physical form.

I was frustrated and my family was feeling the pain. Everything that I had been through was leaking into my body and into my environment.

One cloudy day I recognized that the only one that could make changes in my life was me. I took a different type of action. I hired someone to help me see what I did not see. My journey lasted for years. The one thing I knew was I did not want to keep things pushed down because my body had paid the price and would continue to. I decided the things I had been through in my life were not going to win or determine my future or my family's. I was determined to be the Rockstar I was created to be no matter what had happened in my life. I hope you decide the same thing for yourself.

Go through the next few pages with complete honesty on what is happening in your body and mind.

PHYSICAL

- o Muscle tension/headaches
- o Sleep disturbance/tiredness
- o Skin breakouts
- o Rapid pulse
- o Indigestion
- o Increased sweating
- o Flushing (face feeling hot)
- o Prolonged/Frequent headaches
- o Breathlessness/Chest pain
- o Mild illness
- o Dizziness
- o Ongoing nausea/Stomachache
- o Pain, aches
- o Restless sleep
- o Weight gain or loss
- o Disease
- o Lowered immune system

BEHAVIORAL

o   Appetite changes/Compulsive eating
o   Impatience, carelessness, hyperactivity
o   Poor productivity/Low energy
o   Avoidance of situations or places
o   Change in sleeping patterns
o   Increased alcohol, cigarette, and drug use
o   Increased absenteeism, aggression, irritability
o   Sudden tears
o   Mood swings
o   Hurting self or others

EMOTIONAL

o   Anxiety/Sadness/Suicide
o   Moodiness/Grumpiness
o   Loss of sense of humor
o   Withdrawal/Feeling of isolation
o   Low self- esteem
o   Feelings of guilt and shame
o   Extreme anger (over-reaction)
o   Loss of libido
o   Overwhelming feelings of life

THOUGHTS/PERCEPTION

o   Inability to make decisions
o   Muddled thinking
o   Reduced coordination/creativity
o   Becoming vague/forgetful

o Negative thoughts/Believing everything goes wrong or bad
o Fear of rejection/Defensiveness
o Overly sensitive to criticism
o Poor concentration
o Negative self-talk
o Fear of failure
o Feelings of unfairness
o Can't switch off thoughts

Rockstar Connection:

1. How did you feel after completing this exercise?
2. What did you see as a pattern?
3. How can you make changes right now, so emotions do not affect your body negatively?

JAM SESSION 10

Strong Foundations Create Lasting Change

In this Jam Session, I am diving into how you can build a strong foundation and create lasting change in your life. My goal is to help you create a foundation that will withstand any storm. A strong foundation becomes 10X stronger when you remove the things that have been draining your energy and the weeds in your life that get in the way of being who you were created to be. This allows you to develop who you are to the core and not who others say you are.

It's not easy to do, but I hope with this book you are able to gain the confidence to let go of the things that are not serving you and build the foundation of who you are so you can 10X Your Inner Rockstar. Knowing who you are and learning to manage your emotions is key to being who you were created to be.

Storms are never going to stop coming. You will be tested and sometimes pulled away from who you are, however, when your foundation is set, it is easier to stay the course and come back to your true self time after time. With the right tools and insight, you can make it happen. You have already learned how many thoughts are in your head daily. With that comes emotion, decisions, actions, and reactions. This Jam Session is going to give you a breakdown of some of the components of a sturdy foundation and how they play into managing your emotions and living the life you desire with 100% of who you are.

I have broken down key components of building your foundation. You will notice sub components in some areas.

Emotional Intelligence

Through emotional intelligence you can escape mindlessly reacting to events and emotions by learning to choose your response. Emotional intelligence can develop over time. You must be committed to continued progress toward your life's goals even when the going gets tough. Without a doubt the most important step to improving emotional intelligence is to develop awareness about who you are and how to manage the information that comes into your brain.

Awareness is the Solution

Remember, negative thoughts are often hidden by a positive attitude. From deep inside those conflicting layers, action develops that may not be in alignment with your true self or your true goals. You choose those wrong actions when you have no idea who you are or what motivates you. This disconnect can and often affects your perception of others' behaviors and intentions. Just imagine the problems caused when you act based on misperceptions of your reality and of others' intentions. Most people think that the solution is within the action. WRONG! That is backwards! The solution starts with self-awareness and awareness of others. Once you are aware of who you are, your blind spots, and your biased view of others; the solution will become clear FAST! Taking the RIGHT action is more important than taking action just for the sake of taking action.

Self-Awareness

Self-awareness is the foundation of emotional intelligence and personal growth. It is your ability to perceive your emotions and understand your tendencies in all situations. Self-awareness opens the door to self-regulation which is staying on top of your reactions under stress or in challenging situations. Awareness is key to choosing your response. A high degree of self-awareness requires the willingness to tolerate the discomfort of negative emotions in order to develop and grow.

Go to www.10xYourInnerRockstar.com to measure your Emotional Intelligence and create a plan to improve your emotional understanding of yourself and others.

- **Behaviors**

There are four areas that make up your behavior style. Where you fall on the spectrum of each of the four areas describes HOW you respond to situations and HOW you prefer to engage with others, make decisions, process information, deal with change—basically, how you do everything you do in your life! Recognizing your own behaviors and blind spots is the first step to self-awareness.

Go to www.10xYourInnerRockstar.com to talk with our team. We would love to help you take action and understand your behaviors.

- **Motivators and Driving Forces**

Your internal motivators are something only you know but may not be aware of. Your driving forces indicate WHY you do what you do. When you honor your internal motivators, you have a greater sense of fulfillment and well-being. Motivators fall into six main categories: knowledge, others, surroundings, resources, power, and methodologies. Where you fall on the continuum of each measures your driving forces. Go to www.10xYourInnerRockstar.com if you are ready to find out what is driving you.

- **Strengths**

Have you ever been told to focus on your strengths? How do you know what your strengths are? Most of the time your strengths are covered up by thought distortions. Without knowing where you are strong, you won't know what strengths will help you take action and serve those around you. Maximizing on your unique strengths gives you a clear path to 10Xing Your Inner Rockstar

- **Weaknesses**

Yes, they matter. Weaknesses are what keep your ego in check and constantly growing. They give you areas to develop. We will always be weaker in some areas than others. The key to success is recognizing your weaknesses and either grow it into a strength or delegate it to someone who excels where you don't. Those are the only two choices. Regardless of how you address weaknesses, recognizing and dealing with them helps you be who you were created to be.

- **Tendencies**

What are you most likely to do when faced with expectations? Gretchen Rubin has done important work discovering how internal and external expectations affect people. Knowing your natural tendency gives you great insight into the give and take in your relationships and your ability to stay on course toward achieving the life you want.

- **Intuition**

Your intuition is your inner voice. You know, the one you didn't listen to but wish you had. You naturally have great insight to guide you, but hearing it is difficult because you have built walls to protect yourself. It is important to listen to your internal voice and never invalidate your emotions. You matter. You may have felt insignificant or full of shame all your life. Override those emotions by allowing your internal motivation to push you into positive thoughts or actions. Remember what drives you. Persevere in the face of adversity.

- **Physical Cues**

Pay close attention to your body. This is an important part of self-awareness. Your body can only handle so much. How often you need to recharge or have down time will depend on your behaviors and drivers. We put our body and minds through hell sometimes. Are you a Type A personality or an extrovert who is always in thinking and processing mode? I know I can go at a high-energy level for about six weeks, but then my mind and body will say "Enough. Take a break." I am not depressed. I am normal. I simply need a break. Your body will tell you what you need if you will listen.

Start monitoring what your body tells you daily. When you are stressed, where in your body do you feel it? When do you have the most energy? What time of the day do your emotions begin to change? Most people grow up learning to

83

push their emotions down and away. They never really learn to take cues from their body. Once you start your self-awareness journey and your emotions start to peak, your body will begin to regulate itself and understand what is going on.

Self-Regulation

You can escape mindlessly reacting to events and emotions by learning to choose your response to any given situation. Self-Management requires recognizing and controlling your emotional impulses and what sends you into your Circle of Crazy. Often, we go into the Circle of Crazy because we have a lack of understanding of ourselves and what causes us to react rashly. Road rage is a great example of this behavior. Keep track of your triggers and what sends you into an emotional tailspin. You will notice that the same emotions and the same patterns lead to triggers that set you off. Once you are aware of those, you can take steps to change and manage how you react to the storms that come at you.

- **Circle of Crazy**

Emotions such as fear, guilt, anger, shame, and even loneliness are emotions that keep you in the Circle of Crazy if not controlled. The Circle of Crazy as discussed in Jam Session 6 will come and go. It's when you spot it, are self-aware of what triggers it, and know how to get out of it what matters the most. In my program this is where the most movement happens. To 10X Your Inner Rockstar, you must know how to respond when the Circle of Crazy hits.

84

- **Change Patterns**

Once you begin to feel different, your subconscious brain will want to play tricks on you. Many people think they are depressed. YOU ARE NOT! You may be moving through an emotional cycle, causing almost a depression-like state. This is an absolutely normal process. YOU are OK! Stay strong. Know that during this transition, you may start to feel different or new things. Talk with your coach and keep her updated on any changes in your thoughts and feelings. The imbalances you feel may be due to the recognition of your new belief system at work. Just keep swimming, swimming, swimming!

Relationship or Others' Awareness

Learn to relate to others in an empathetic way. Meet people where they are emotionally without jumping into their Circle of Crazy or inviting them into yours. When you react to others in a negative way, they are winning. That does not mean you won't be mad but allow it to get you into action and not reaction. Most people relate to others through projection of their own needs. Maintaining control over your own emotions and having empathy for the other person will help you build solid relationships. Acknowledge their pain, try to understand their situation, and love them anyway, without feedback. You only know 2% of what someone has going on and they only know 2% of what you have going on.

Don't jump into the assuming game. You have lifetime of shit that has happened to you, and they have a lifetime of shit that has happened to them. All that shit piled up just

85

makes relationships messy. Some people will trigger you and you will trigger some people. Most of the time it has nothing to do with each other and has everything to do with how each of you process what is coming through your lens.

Emotional Intelligence Begins with Discovering U – Your Internal Inventory

In my programs Internal Inventory is covered in the Discovering U and Developing U courses. Once you have discovered and removed all the weeds that are stealing from you and your life, you can now spend your energy to developing you. When you choose to take this journey to be who you were created to be, life happens the way you always dreamed. That doesn't mean stuff won't come up or you won't experience chaos. The challenges of life never stop coming. The one thing you have is YOU. Being the best parent, business leader, doctor, or coach starts with YOU. You will have a solid foundation and be able to make a real impact on those around you. You were born into a world that was full of other people's beliefs and stories.

Sometimes that is good and sometimes it is not. It's either serving you or taking away. Your internal inventory is knowing you: your strengths, your weaknesses, your motivators, behaviors, tendencies, etc. Once you have a full understanding of who you are, you see the right action with clarity. Knowing your internal inventory helps you 10X Your Inner Rockstar. If you feel like other programs have not worked for you in the past, this could be why. You must do all things according to your internal inventory.

Your dreams and goals become your reality only when built on a strong foundation of self-awareness and the other parts of emotional intelligence. In other words, your foundation matters! If we build a house without a strong foundation, it would fall. The same is true for you and your goals and dreams. My ROCKSTAR team and I have put together special resources for you that will help you solidify your position as a Rockstar.

Go to www.10xYourInnerRockstar.com to learn more.

In Summary

In my programs we take you through the process of Discovering U and Developing U, a step-by-step process of developing self-awareness. I feel like this is what most personal growth programs are missing. It is imperative that you understand why you do what you do, become self-aware about how you react to things within you and around you, recognize and understand your emotions and where they come from because that gives you POWER over your life and helps you 10X Your Inner Rockstar.

Understand this: Only a small percentage of people in this world can control their emotions, but you can be one of them!

"Men and women are not prisoners of their fate, but only prisoners of their own minds"

-Franklin D. Roosevelt

Rockstar Connection:

1. How well do you know your body and mind? When is the most productive part of your day? When do you feel the most energetic? Where do you feel the most inspired? Are there certain times of the day, circumstances or places that make it hard for you to focus and get things done?

> Go to www.10xYourInnerRockstar.com to measure your Emotional Intelligence and create a plan to improve your understanding of yourself and others.

2. What are your primary behaviors? What drives you or motivates you?
3. You can take control of your destiny once you realize that your power lies in your ability to choose your thoughts and then your actions. What kind of thoughts do you typically give energy and priority to in the course of your day? Are they constructive? Are they true? Do they move you toward your mission of being all you can be?

JAM SESSION 11

The Emotional Connection

Now that you are aware of what is happening with your emotions and in your life, it's time to make the real connection. You may have had breakthroughs, you may be more aware, your relationships could look different at this point, or you could be trying to process all of this stuff in your head. I have seen people come into my program and after just three sessions, their lives are changed forever in a dramatic way. The principles I teach get results fast. Action happens. Embrace wherever you are in this journey after reading this book.

It is possible that you could go into what I call the over-thinking brain and be magnifying the stories in your head. Depending on your behavior style, this could be a very real thing for you. This Jam Session will help you make the connection so you can slow down, simplify, and get out of your over-thinking brain. I want you to go confidently into the next season of your life as an action-taker who is focused on living a Rockstar life. I want you to Take Action Fearlessly. You will experience a shift. It could take 1 day or 6 months – only you know. It is important to let your body and mind process and to take the time you need. Your head and your heart are trying to connect.

I have summarized some of the most important things you need to remember on this journey. Read them below and answer the questions in Rockstar Connection truthfully.

Protective Walls Rewritten

You may have heard that it's good to drop your walls. I disagree. Keep them up. Your walls have been formed for a reason. They are meant to protect you. They only thing that I want you to change or be aware of is if they are hurting you or helping you. Some protective walls may not be serving you because of your blind spots. Use the tools from this book to help you discover if your protective walls are helping to develop Your Inner Rockstar or holding it back.

Patterns Overflowing

You may have patterns in your life that have played out since you were a baby. It is best to slow down and define what they are and whether they are hurting or helping. You are the only one that can decide that.

Emotions Serve a Purpose

Emotions are reactions to our life experience. They developed to serve a purpose – to protect you. However, what once was beneficial and necessary can be limiting your progress without your realizing it.

Making a Shift

When your belief system starts to shift, you will notice that your self-awareness tools kick in, and you can tolerate negative emotions, challenges, and events more effectively.

Getting into Action

The only way to understand your emotions is to spend time thinking through them and figuring out where they come from and why they are there. Emotions can come from anywhere and they get action/reaction out of you, good, bad, or indifferent.

Peeling Back

Emotions are like onions. You peel back the layers of your emotions, becoming more and more comfortable with who you are at the core. This will allow you to discover your true self. This is your head and heart connecting.

Facing the Truth

Who you are can be scary. It takes an extreme amount of courage and honesty. You can no longer hide when you become self-aware. You will learn to use your voice, stand up, and fight for who you are and what you offer this world. If you are mad, then be mad. If you are sad, then be sad. Just make sure your actions are serving you rather than inhibiting you.

Becoming Aware

As you become more aware of your emotions, start discovering how to manage them. Get to the core of issues quickly and process them. But at the same time, keep in mind that if strong emotions have surfaced, the situation deserves a delayed response. This is a good strategy to keep you from doing something you will regret later. It also teaches you managing skills that you need to know going forward. Self-awareness is not about discovering your deepest secrets. Rather, it is a straightforward, honest way to help you know who you are and what makes you tick. Understanding what you do well helps to motivate and inspire you, which will lead to personal fulfillment.

Certain Triggers

Situations can and will push your buttons and trigger you. Self-awareness helps you improve your skills. Start by knowing what your autopilot reaction is when your buttons are pushed, and you are triggered. When you are triggered and perceive a negative emotion, listen and seek to improve.

Emotional Mistakes

There are not any mistakes in life when you understand who you are and what you want. You will fail but failure teaches us. Don't be afraid of your emotional mistakes and failures. Embrace your knowledge and insight because of those things. When you are self-aware and believe in who you are, I promise you will pursue the right opportunities. Put your strengths to work and keep your emotions from holding you back.

Develop your Character

We tend to embrace things that make us comfortable and shy away from things that make us uncomfortable. This can cause us to miss opportunities to develop our character. We must stretch and grow to be emotionally healthy. The more we understand both our beauty and our blemishes, the better we can achieve our full potential.

Rockstar Connection:

1. Do you feel like your emotions are serving you to 10X Your Inner Rockstar?
2. Have you felt a shift in your life and belief about who you are? If not, Why? If yes, what has shifted, and what did you do to get there?
3. What layers are you peeling back? How is peeling back those layers serving you, and what do you want to accomplish in life?
4. Do you feel like you have a voice and are ready to stand up and fight for who you are?
5. What are you learning about you?

JAM SESSION 12

It's time! It is time to Take Action and be who you were created to be. You were created to be a 10. You were created to live a life full of joy and happiness. Storms won't stop coming. That's life. You need to learn to dance in the rain and decide NEVER to let the storms, the chaos, the experiences, and the circumstances STEAL from you or from the 10 you were created to be. No matter if it's your story or a diagnosis that you did not ask for – no matter what, you are a 10. If you feel anything less than a 10, you have things stealing from you and renting space in the beautiful brain that you have been given. I know it's not easy, but you can do this. Today, I want you to declare you have a voice over your life. Declare you are standing up and taking charge of taking the action that will serve who you were created to be. I am all about action. It's who I am. In this Jam Session you have simple action steps that will move you from allowing things to rent space in your head to taking action fearlessly.

Pull the Weeds

Get rid of what's not serving you. It's not easy. YOU know better than anyone else what keeps you from taking action.

Quit Invalidating HOW You Feel.

Don't invalidate your emotions. All emotions are there to help you understand who you are. Every emotion that we have can teach us something. It is how we move forward with that emotional information that matters most.

Take Note How Your Emotions Affect Others

It is important to understand how your emotions affect other people. Take some time to process how you behave towards others and around them. The more you understand how your emotions affect others, the better equipped you will become giving you a choice on what kind of impact you want to have on people.

Don't Avoid or Ignore

Don't avoid your emotions. When you learn to lean into what hurts you, then you will learn to use that emotion by doing something productive with it. Ignoring the feeling does not make it go away. Emotions will surface again when you least expect it, causing you to question who you are and pulling you into victim mode. Don't be afraid of emotional mistakes. They can serve as great opportunities for you to grow and develop. Remember that your brain can play tricks on you!

Welcome Your Emotions with Open Arms

You must learn to feel your emotions, determine if they are legitimate or not, and then make a decision to act in a healthy way. Remember that your mind and nerve system are tightly connected. If you hold negative emotions in your body, they can cause stress, disease, and health concerns throughout your entire system. It can also lead to the trap of using drugs, alcohol, food, TV, social media, sex, or other types of addiction to suppress or numb the pain. Own your emotions – just don't let them control you!

Know Who and What Triggers You

Knowing your triggers will keep your emotions from sending you into the Circle of Crazy. Take notes and jot down things that make you mad, frustrated, or just straight up angry. A good coach can help you process through those if you need help.

Watch Yourself

Sometimes when emotions come at us so fast, we tend to overreact to a situation. That happens suddenly, and we blow up. Watch yourself closely and learn to take advantage of the calm before the storm. You may become angry, sad, or lonely in a weak moment. This is when excuses start to come out. In any situation, you are likely to get better results when you stay emotionally sound. Your anger will not make anyone change. Rationally explaining things with calm emotions will create the change you want.

Brain Dump Your Emotions

It's hard to develop a perspective on your emotions and tendencies when everyday feels like a new mountain to climb. Journaling your emotions helps you to get things out of your mind. It also helps to keep your mind from trying to process so much at one time. And finally, it helps you to remember the emotions that have been dug up, allowing you to process them yourself or with your coach. Make this a PRIORITY.

97

Don't Be Fooled by a Bad Mood

Being in a bad mood is just part of life. It can be corrected easily, even though it does not seem like it sometimes. When that bad mood sets in, the first thing you will need to do is to admit that you are in a bad mood. Then allow yourself to stop trying to be something you aren't. It's okay to have these days. They will teach you valuable lessons, but it is also important to know that just saying the word REWIND can refresh what is happening. Take a 10-minute break and turn on upbeat music to reset your mood. One tool that I highly recommend to my clients is for them to use their "I AM" statement that we have developed together (this is a statement that reflects a healthy version of who you are). Say it often to remind yourself who you are and what you offer this world.

Don't Be Fooled by a Good Mood

Being excited and in a good mood can lead to trouble if you are not careful. You should always strive to make decisions wisely and in a calm and deliberate manner (not in a low or high emotional state).

Acknowledge Why You Do What You Do

Your self-awareness will grow abundantly when you begin seeking out the source of your feelings. It may not seem like it at first, but staying on course, even when it gets hard, is key to your growth process. Emotions serve an important purpose. They key you into things you never understood and help you understand yourself better. Tracing your emotions back to their origins will give you clarity, peace, and insight into the different things happening or not happening in your life. The more equipped you become to understand your emotions, the better you will become about managing your emotions and living in peace.

Know Your Values, Your Mission, and Your I AM Statement

These are the most important components of personal growth. Things will come up that will test you against who you really are. Visiting these two components daily will keep you moving in the right direction. Your coach will help you to write a mission statement for your life. This will help you feel alive every day. When your life aligns with your I AM statement, your values, and your mission, you will start to feel complete.

Go to www.10xYourInnerRockstar.com for information on how to create your own I AM statement.

Spot Your Mood in the Environment

This can and will change any mood. You can also read and listen to things that fuel your mind and soul. If you have a hurdle to get over, a sad movie can sometimes do the trick. Just know what you need when you need it.

Seek Feedback

Self-awareness is the process of getting to know yourself from the inside out. Getting feedback is key. However, make sure your feedback is coming from a sound influence and trusted source. Otherwise, you may be getting information from someone in his or her own Circle of Crazy. If you want to grow, get advice that will move you forward, not send you backward.

Be Socially Aware

Be able to recognize emotions in other people and understand what is going on even when you are right in the middle of it. You can stay focused and keep your emotions in check without letting the emotions of others negatively affect you.

Get to Know Yourself in Your Circle of Crazy

Get to know yourself and your body. Understand stress and stay ahead of the game. Stress can cause many health concerns and emotions that are not necessary. Emotions go deep. They can give you headaches, stomach issues, heart concerns, and much more. When you can recognize stress, you can recharge your batteries by partnering with a doctor that specializes in upper cervical care. This will help to open your body, reset your power, process your emotions, and have your body functioning properly on all levels.

Stop Searching

Put down all those darn books, podcasts, and seminars that you think will give you the answers. YES, those things are important. Those things are needed BUT not if they keep you from taking action. Too often people rely on the external things to give them answers. If you slow down your brain for just a short time, the answers may come. God can't get in if your brain is in constant chaos. Turn it off, listen, and be still. Get some down time in.

Jump in and TAKE ACTION!

1. Are you ready to stop measuring your emotions and jump into action?

   If yes, great! Let's goooooo!

   If not, what emotions or circumstance are holding you back?

2. Are you diving into your discomfort or are you holding on to something that is keeping you from 10Xing Your Inner Rockstar?

3. Do your values and mission align with who you are and what you want to accomplish in life?

   If so, what's next for you?

   If not, what do you need to do to get into alignment?

4. Are your emotions affecting others, and have you learned to manage them through this process?

   If so, what has changed for you?

   If not, what needs to change?

5. Are you ready to declare that you are going to 10X Your Inner Rockstar?

   If so, move on to the ENERGY SHOTS and begin your journey!

If not, why? What is holding you back?

If you have come to this point and need help on this journey, please reach out to us so we can help you 10X Your Inner Rockstar!

JAM SESSION 13

You are now writing *your* own story. You are in the midst of taking control of your emotions to be the Rockstar YOU were created to be. Read these Energy Shots, take note of them, use them daily to push you. Write your own Energy Shots. You are your own Rockstar. YOU are 10Xing Your Inner Rockstar. This is not about me or the people around you. It's about what you need and how you are energizing yourself. Once you revive your energy and 10X Your Inner Rockstar, you will be 100% for the people around you.

- Stay consistent with your mentor, coach, or community. If you are feeling better, make sure you know why and have noted what has been the catalyst that helped you. Never give up on something that has given you positive results--even if it hurts a little!
- Expect progress, not perfection. I know it's hard. Put down the red pencil and stop grading yourself. More than likely, no one else is either.
- Be patient, stop rushing, stop taking things so seriously. Go right now and watch a little TV, go hiking, pick up your guitar, or consider doing something you have NEVER done.
- Stay focused no matter how hard the journey gets. Sorry to tell you this, but storms will NEVER stop coming. But they will get easier to handle and you may even learn to "dance in the rain."

- If you are unable to move forward, stop thinking. Just jump! Stop analyzing and looking for more details. They will come eventually. JUST JUMP! Take constructive action. Even if you fail, it will be an opportunity to learn.
- Stop lying to yourself. Everything is not always okay, and you are not the only one with problems. Lean in to gain understanding.
- If you have a dream, GO after it! Stop listening to other people, and trust who you were created to be. You are unique and beautiful.

JAM SESSION 14

Be courageous. Act on your belief that all people were created to be ROCKSTARS. Understand that life happens. It's your job to lean in, to take responsibility, and to clear the clutter in your head, so you can have the life you want. You are not your circumstances. Spend your time challenging your excuses and your story and Take Action Fearlessly.

Live a life full of passion and driven by mission. You have choices. You always have choices. You can choose happiness. Know that everyone makes mistakes and will continue to. What matters is how you let it affect you. Believe deeply that everyone is unique and should be celebrated. Do what it takes to live life to the fullest without letting people or circumstances drag you down. Focus on what's important. Work hard to create the life of your dreams.

Live life to the fullest by maximizing your God-given talent without compromising your values or integrity. Do not focus on pleasing others or meeting their expectations. Rather, aim to declutter, develop, and strengthen yourself so you can be the best version of you to be the best for the people around you.

Do not focus on the negative or listen to the haters who are self-projecting and living in their Circle of Crazy. Stand tall and smile when the storms come and go. Believe in possibilities. Understand that emotions and failures are part of life and present opportunities to learn and grow.

TAKE ACTION FEARLESSLY.

WALK THROUGH FEAR.

LEARN TO DANCE IN THE RAIN.

**NEVER COMPROMISE WHO YOU ARE
FOR ANYONE OR ANYBODY.**

YOU are in control of your own destiny, your response, your future, and your results. Choose to Be the Rockstar You Were Created to Be!

YOU ARE A ROCKSTAR!

JAM SESSION 15

Let's 10X Your Inner Rockstar

What Kind of Rockstar Do You Want to Be?

You have done the work, and our hope is that you have Unlocked the Power of Your Emotions and are ready to Take Action Fearlessly.

It is time to take it one step further and be the Rockstar you were created to be. It is time to uncover that Rockstar inside of you.

We have resources waiting for you.

Go to 10xYourInnerRockstar.com and take your very own 10X assessment and schedule a Mini Rockstar Session to help you take the next step.

When you do you will receive a Free gift that will help you be committed to yourself.

JAM SESSION 16

The Final Jam Session

Our Final Jam Session is full of stories of ordinary people just like you who decided to take a step and to 10X their Inner Rockstar. These people have been positively impacted by my program. I believe very strongly that this page must be authentic and true. The testimonials have NOT been modified in any way. I want you to feel the real weight of the words of people who have been deeply healed and helped by my program (their stories have been added here with their permission). Every story on this page is uniquely different. Each has started the journey to 10X his or her Inner Rockstar.

We are eager to hear your story! If you have attended an event, been engaged in my program, or have been impacted by me in any way, please email us your impact story at Impact@10xYourInnerRockstar.com We would love to share your story and pay it forward to millions of other people giving them hope and showing them all that is possible!

Impact Stories

When I met Leisa, my emotional life was an out of control. She gave me the proper tools to help me get in control of my life again. I have been using her strategies for over three years now!

Since then, I have been able to keep my composure during stressful times, grow richer in happiness, and help others at a higher level.

Leisa is an amazing coach that will meet you on your level and help you move forward in your life! She is for real!

Thank you Leisa for helping me break old patterns, dump the baggage and create a new life story!!!

Dr. Nick Hagan

My challenge was letting go and moving on to who I really wanted to be. Loving myself was the challenge and believing that I could be happy without my current relationship. Having the courage to trust God and let him guide my life.

My biggest wins came from working with Leisa. I quit smoking!!! Started a new life in Florida and opening Pearle Vision franchises!!!

Leisa was my guiding force that gave me the guidance and courage to live life to the fullest. Leisa is the best Life Coach anyone could bring into their life. She helped me become a Rockstar!!

Susan Erker

Leisa came into my life at the exact right moment. As a young mom trying to grow a business, I was looking for someone who could help me overcome my limiting beliefs and manage what Leisa calls the Circle of Crazy.

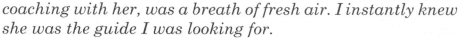

Our first meeting, which was before I had decided to do coaching with her, was a breath of fresh air. I instantly knew she was the guide I was looking for.

Leisa has been there every step of the way helping me define my values, my goals and create action items for me to focus on. Is my life still crazy? Yes! But I am better equipped to handle the crazy. I understand my emotions and motivations better and I am learning to manage my life and business instead of having life manage me. You will not be disappointed by deciding to hire Leisa.

She is wise beyond her years, caring, compassionate and sincere.

Spencer A.

"We hired Leisa Jenkins to help us work through some very serious family and relationship issues. It is difficult to put into words the tremendous impact for good that Leisa has had on our lives. We joke that she is an angel sent from heaven just when we needed one most!

Leisa has the uncanny ability to identify the core, the root of an issue almost immediately. And she then has the solution. It may be hard work to put that solution into play, but it is the only way to make the change that is so desperately needed. She has never once steered us in anything but the right direction.

Leisa Jenkins is a problem solver. This is her gift. She sees the problem, names it, then explains how to tackle it in a practical, common sense, respectful and loving way.

If you are not interested in changing then forget it because she is all about getting you out of the rut in which you are stuck and on to a healthy, whole, success filled and happier place in life. Whatever the challenge I believe Leisa Jenkins can figure it out!

Dan & Betsy K

I have enjoyed working with Leisa Jenkins over the last year. I have learned so much about myself, my spouse and even my coworkers. The way she breaks it down for me and helps me see whatever it is we are discussing from the other-side has been a great help.

She shares other theories, gives me the reasoning of why people, including myself, do what they do and gets me out of my own head so I can make better decisions. Knowing all of that information makes life a lot clearer.

My head chatter is gone, and my actions are more on target of what my goals are. Most importantly all my relationships (family, friends, coworkers and the one with myself) are better for having her in my life. She is a straight shooter that you can confide in and trust.

Dianne Collins

THANK YOU
FOR SHOWING UP
FOR YOURSELF

Join Us

Did you love this book? Please share this with others and help us change the world one person at a time!

What's next for you? Join Rockstar U and continue to Take Action and be the Rockstar you were created to be!

Apply for your 30-minute Impact Session by going to www.10xYourInnerRockstar.com

ABOUT OUR COMPANY

We believe in you!

Our company was designed to help you move from where you have been and where you are right now to where you want to go. We have helped thousands of people declutter their lives and Take Action.

Life is full of sacrifices, challenges, obstacles, and storms. We promise to walk beside you and support you through the storms of life so that you can 10X Your Inner Rockstar and live the life you were created to live.

We will never give up on YOU!

Emma's Story

I am going to tell you a story very near to my heart. This section is dedicated to my daughter who has been a fighter since the moment she was born. She fought to be who she was created to be but lost that desire through experience, circumstance, opinions, and unanswered questions.

Emma's story started before she was born. She was our only planned child out of four. Crazy right! Why does this matter? It took one year and six long months to conceive her. I used to blame myself for some of the craziness you will hear. Why did I try so hard? Did my emotions cause this? Was I forcing nature? What did I do wrong? It was an emotional journey.

The baby we wanted so bad was born with a journey filled with chaos. She was born in 2003 in a hospital room where she was determined to make a big entrance. She didn't even wait for the doctor. I was in pain one minute, and the next minute her dad was catching her in his arms while the nurse was screaming for help. Born four weeks early at 5 pounds 9 ounces with jaundice. Emma was a restless baby and could never get comfortable. On a routine visit at three months old, our absolute favorite doctor noticed the left side of Emma's belly was swollen. She was rushed to the hospital for surgery on her left kidney.

119

Every few weeks after that we were in the hospital with high fevers, overnight stays, spinal taps, and tests.

The next 16 years was full of health scares and overnight hospital stays. Emma has had her fair share of doctors and opinions. She created a tough shell and felt like everything was her fault: her health, her anxiety, her cautious nature. We searched and searched for answers. I knew that something was not right, but no one would listen. They blamed it on her weight making us seem like the worst parents out there. Emma developed a perception that no one could help her and was consumed with negative thoughts, internalized emotions, and feelings of hopelessness. She lost hope that she could live the life she was created for.

As a mom watching this happen from the outside, you can only pray and support her the best you know how. But I worried. I am human. I lost sleep and fought to find the answers.

In September of 2018, we had had enough. I called a friend who was a doctor and said we needed help. I filled her in and scheduled an appointment. We went in with hope but also with protective walls that this could be just another doctor telling us what we had already heard so many times before.

As the doctor conducted a routine ultrasound, we waited patiently for the results in her office. The door opened and my heart sank--you know the crazy mom internal feeling. I knew in my heart that we would have answers. She sat down and started to tell us that Emma's ovaries were not working. She was in a menopausal state.

She moved on to the doctor science talk. Over-our-head words and phrases that really meant nothing. Her conclusion was that we would have to run more tests and that would take weeks.

Lost in the details, we just sat there. We did not know enough to ask questions but only enough to make assumptions. The doctor stopped and looked at Emma with emotion and understanding and said, "none of this is your fault." For the first time my little girl cried. Her life was changed in that very moment. And while that was only the start of the next season, we had waited 16 years for answers, and they were finally coming. There was a mix of emotions: fear, hope, and peace.

We had a second wind but that would not come without more chaos. After two weeks of waiting, I received the call. The call that would tell us what we are really facing. I was sitting in a client's house as my phone rang. I excused myself from the meeting took the call and as my eyes filled with tears and my emotions were all over the place. I was trying to hold it together but it was too much. I was told my daughter had Turner syndrome.

A syndrome that only 1 in 2000 girls are diagnosed with. Finally, the answer to why we spent restless nights worrying, why she had high fevers and no answers. On the other end of the phone, I hear the words *"Leisa the next few months are going to be hectic and stressful, but I promise you that it will get better."* Oh man, she was right. The journey was hard. We cried a lot. But, *and hear me on this*, WE HAD ANSWERS.

No doctors could tell us what was going on – not in 16 years of asking. No real answers. People can lose themselves after fighting for so long and feeling defeated. I don't believe that people don't want to get better; I believe that people are lost just like our Emma was.

We are not blaming the doctors but a lot of doctors out there are just not educated about Turners. They did not know what to test for. WE BELIEVE THAT!

There are three reasons I am telling you my daughter's story:

#1 – It takes one person to change your life - just one. The one for us was Dr. Levey. An OB-GYN who listened and heard our cries. Don't ever give up. Keep searching, keep fighting, keep taking action fearlessly. That is the best way to find that one person who will hear you. I PROMISE!

#2 – Just like my clients' stories, my story, my daughter's story, and the millions of others out there that have a diagnosis to deal with, the story of perseverance is real. You always have the choice to push through and be who you were created to be. No matter what life delivers, YOU CAN 10X Your Inner Rockstar. Emma was not just a lucky child. She has been a fighter and, yes, she had some bad days, but she never gave up. We fought for her life. I fought for mine, and you can too.

#3 – We totally and completely support the Turner Syndrome Foundation. We have partnered with them because our passion is to support other Turner girls. We want to make people aware of Turner syndrome.

The Turner Syndrome Foundation needs our support, not just for my daughter, but for the thousands of girls dealing with this. Some are scared of what this means for them, and some are hiding because they don't know how to deal with it. Others feel like they have no one to talk with and their parents feel unsupported and alone. Doctors are scrambling to be educated on Turner syndrome. We need to get the word out there is help and support. My Emma is a miracle child.

If a child is diagnosed in the womb, the common suggestion is to abort the baby because most pregnancies with TS end in miscarriage anyway, and if they do survive, no one knows what the child could face growing up. However, Emma made it. She is a very healthy young woman living her life and 10Xing her inner rockstar. I promise you can too – no matter what comes your way.

Help us reach the world so that everyone has the chance to be who they were created to be!

**To learn more about Turner Syndrome
go to: www.TSFUSA.org**

To hear more about Emma's story watch this video

Turner Syndrome affects 1 in 2,000 females.

The goal of the Turner Syndrome Foundation (TSF) is to support research initiatives and develop educational programs to increase professional awareness and enhance medical care of those affected by Turner Syndrome.

Early diagnosis and comprehensive treatments over the lifespan will lead to a brighter and healthier future for all young girls and women with Turner Syndrome.

TSF is a registered 501(c)(3) organization incorporated in New Jersey

Made in the USA
Middletown, DE
08 March 2020